Hope's Embrace

And Other Poems

2nd Edition

A. K. Frailey

The Writings of A. K. Frailey

Books for the Mind and Spirit

https://akfrailey.com/

Contact

akfrailey@yahoo.com

Historical Science Fiction Novels

OldEarth ARAM Encounter

OldEarth Ishtar Encounter

OldEarth Neb Encounter

OldEarth Georgios Encounter

OldEarth Melchior Encounter

Science Fiction Novels

Homestead

Last of Her Kind

Newearth Justine Awakens

Newearth A Hero's Crime

Short Stories

It Might Have Been—And Other Short Stories 2nd Edition

One Day at a Time and Other Stories

*Encounter Science Fiction
Short Stories & Novella 2nd Edition*

Inspirational Non-Fiction

*My Road Goes Ever On—
Spiritual Being, Human Journey 2nd Edition*

My Road Goes Ever On—A Timeless Journey

The Road Goes Ever On—

A Christian Journey Through The Lord of the Rings

Children's Book

The Adventures of Tally-Ho

Poetry

Hope's Embrace & Other Poems 2nd Edition

**Audible Versions are now available.
Check book details on Amazon for
current listings.**

Contents

Introduction

When I was a senior in college, I took a creative writing class. To my dismay, I was informed that rhymes were quite out of fashion, though disconcertingly, the best writer in the class wrote only in rhyming prose. But I did get one brilliant piece of advice from the young and earnest professor: Write what you mean.

A great idea that rings with biblical truth.

All I had to do was figure out what I meant. What anything or anyone meant. To me. To the universe.

I wrote very little after that. None of it good.

Instead, I figured that I would go ahead and live my life, and maybe I'd figure out "meaning" along the way. Kind of like learning to drive. I took driver's ed in school, but it was really road trips that taught me how to handle a car.

After moving to various cities and towns, interacting with a spectrum of individuals, enjoying new experiences, suffering hurt and loss, I discovered that I didn't know all that much. Family, friends, and perfect strangers have always been happy to correct my vast ignorance on a whole host of issues.

Writing came to me in stages. I practiced doing it wrong for quite a while, then tried some new variations, and in recent years, I've seen some improvement. I'd like to stay on that upward trend.

But poetry has always been in a class by itself. I bucked the system from the get-go. Rhymes work for me. I like their feel and sound. I enjoy

the challenge of finding a word to rhyme with...that actually fits with my theme. But, most importantly, I like how poems mean something even when they appear to be hanging upside down from a tree branch.

I love the sensation that in a poem, I can't really be wrong or out of style, stupid or ignorant. I'm simply seeing. Feeling. Living through words.

Though Flannery O'Connor made a valid point when she said that sometimes teachers don't stifle writers enough, there is a certain rightness to my college professor's premise. Writing what I mean has never been the hard part. Living my meaning and then writing about it—now there's a challenge.

Hope's Embrace

A Bhuaci Poem

Originally published on
The Writings of A. K. Frailey 3/10/2017

Sisters—linking arms amid the crashing seas-breeze

waves—laughing as we fell,

For we knew no fear in our homeland—there we did

happily dwell.

Hope ever sprouted,

Love never doubted.

When invaders destroyed our youth and ships to far stars

were sent,

Still, our hearts beat true to love—to our faith's content.

You on board, shivering and afraid,

Me, left behind to protect the homeworld, where I stayed.

Long years passed and messages did tell of new homes fair,

I wish I'd been with you and every adventure shared.

But my content was in knowing you were free,

For enduring great danger here, never safe were we.

Strange silence then ensued and fearful the cause we pursued.

No words can describe the loss—an entire planet laid waste.

Only dead rocks floating in space—a home—myriad dreams erased.

So sister now, only memory serves to fill the aching void,

Where once we played and with our lives enjoyed.

But somber truth teaches—even in heavy loss we endure,

To strengthen that which is beyond any mortal cure.

My daughter now I send—to far distant stars to seek,

Our salvation in a future none yet can hope to speak.

My child, cling fast to the dream that held us in its sway,

The joys and laughter that brighten youth's holy,

every-day.

For there is no salvation found apart from the dreams that

dwell,

Safely in the hearts of those who love so well.

GO ON
Originally published on
The Writings of A. K. Frailey 4/18/2017

Winter never came,
Spring came too soon.
Summer came and burned us up,
Autumn's hope from doom.

Childhood raced me by,
Grown-up came too soon.
Parenthood came and livened things up,
Ancient wisdom is my future bloom.

I live upon the seasons, God,
Seasons come and go.
So fast, oh God, so fast.

We yearn, we long,
We freeze, we burn,
We change as seasons go.

Forgive us, Lord,
We forget; we long for seasons gone.
Give us this day our daily bread.
Look and see the leaves fall and freeze,

Then, oh God, the spring breeze.
Go on—go on.

Truth of Loveliness

Originally published on
The Writings of A. K. Frailey 7/12/2017

As dappled light crawls up the trees,
The sun sets slanting across the seas.

Children murmur in evening play,
Birds chirp goodnight to the day.

Staccato hoots of an early owl,
Cats wander on the prowl.

The breeze stills,
The air chills.

The last tractor rumbles by,
Piano chords through open windows sigh.

Fireflies flash their fairy lights,
Frogs chorus into the night.

Sweet is the summer evening fair,
When life and love and joy do dare,

To accomplish that which no earthly
treasure buys,
A truth of loveliness that never dies.

Soul's Birth in Morning Soil
Originally published on
The Writings of A. K. Frailey 10/4/2017

Soul's birth in morning soil,

Spring sprouts from ancient toil.

First steps — firm hold to fingertip,

Grace flows from humble village to ocean ships.

Learning, spinning — webs of life,

Heavenly rays over world-weary strife.

Burdens heavy lay,

Under heat of summer day.

Teacher, prophet, counselor — grief overcome,

Waning light, shortened day — whispers a weakened
sun.

Age lines, gray hair, gathering fate,

Autumn harvest — profits wait.

Family tree beyond the page,

Humble grains on winter days.

Souls rebirth in Heaven's glory,

Sings of God's unending story.

Winter's Irony

Originally published on
The Writings of A. K. Frailey 1/5/2018

Barren branches against a pregnant sky,
Rustling leaves only sigh.

Soft flakes fall upon a hard ground,
In multitudes—without a sound.

Frozen blanket of icy snow,
Warm the burrows of those below.

Chilled bones hinder the will,
Yet glories roam the landscape still.

Ponder beauty from above,
As echoes mirror ancient love.

Unwelcoming winter may be,
Bringing joy, our eyes to see.

Ironic season of buried dreams,
Awakens our souls to hope unseen.

To See Another Day

Originally published on
The Writings of A. K. Frailey 6/21/2018

Summer's glory not,
Battles ever fought.

Garden seeds and springing weeds,
Speak of endless deeds.

Joy-filled fun,
Wearies under the blistering sun.

Insects buzz and bite,
Never a moment's respite.

Yet dew-sparkled webs amid the grassy green,
Offer light-hearted beauty, joy in being.

Birds greet the sun, soak in glorious rays,
Encouraging buzzing bees—at the brink of day.

Dark gloom forgot,
As season's blooms brought,

Vibrant color taught,
Old hearts in beauty caught.

Summer's glory be,
The moon's radiance see.

Fruits and fauns, yellow daffodils,
Invigorated limbs and nurtured wills.

Seasons pass through many a trial,
Growing life through every heart-filled mile.

Journey each we may,
Hope to see another day.

ALL HUMANITY

Originally published on The Writings of A. K. Frailey
9/28/2018

An empty bench waits by the sea,

Ponder time and silence free.

Loving son and loving daughter,

Blue sky and bluer sea.

Dragonflies flitter by,

The waves roll on a mid-day sigh.

Sand, rock, weed, and flower,

Nature changes by the hour.

All our name and titles float away,

Petty divisions hate of the day.

Only myself, yet everyone be,

Join in communion with all humanity.

Long Journey

Originally published on The Writings of A. K. Frailey
12/1/2020

Climbing unimagined height,

Soul wearies,

Cold, relentless wind does bite.

Family clan, broken shell,

Seeking love in seeking friend,

Beauty finds

Truth doesn't bend.

Clamoring gong, attention now,

Sweet good nature the Earth does plow.

Tree lines fall, alone on high.

The valley spread in glory, sigh.

Hand in hand, heart to heart,

Living, serving, company apart.

God in majesty does hand out reach

Holding faith, experience teach.

Pinnacle—Human-divine

Love lost?

Never mine.

Vision Flight

Originally published on The Writings of A. K. Frailey
12/15/20

Swaying branch,

Autumn day,

Bright sun,

Blue way.

Thoughts unsettled.

Rambling

Aimless

Noontime crest,

Sameness blest.

Craving nest, comfort snuggle,

Homestead Heartstead

Faith, please double!

Waiting through sunlight,

Brazen Hopelight,

God's own Surenight.

Twilight

Promise

All in shadow

Home

Distant Meadow

Vision flight, fading light exclaim,

No lonely center,

Separate souls' bane.

Unity

Intimacy

Bare

Nurture

Service

17

Share

Highest sun, lowest dare,

No fantom dream,

But honest glare.

Imperfect light,

See we,

Most Perfect Sight.

Remember

Originally published on The Writings of A. K. Frailey
12/29/2020

The wonder of a child's stare,
As once we climbed a tree on dare.

The humming, buzzing bee,
Ourselves did marvel at flurry-wings see.

Sharp green apples snatched,
High branches, contentment wrapped.

Unleashed from class,
Homeward dash.

Friends to play,
Blazing trails to stray.

Holiday fun-arranged,
Presents-exchanged.

Growing, planning, hoping, for my sake,
Dreaming awake.

Passion driven,
Conscience striven.

A world of
Could be...
Should be...

Remember,
Youth's promise,

When old-age,
Experience,
Pain and loss,
Strew life behind,

Remember,
And climb.

Genius Love from Above

Originally published on The Writings of A. K. Frailey
1/21/2021

My head is stuffed with thoughts profound,

The puppy's eyes follow me round.

From cradle to grave,

My brilliance—a knave.

To-do lists organize life,

Duty calls for thrifty wife.

Family, friends, country, space,

A universe of relations

Olympic race.

Mom's wisdom,

Not so wise.

Answers have not,

Compliance rot.

Trade texts for text,

Offer emoji smile.

So little a thing,

Happiness bring.

Genius love,

From above.

Grace endows a simple heart,

This world to next, we never part.

For Goodness Sake

Originally published on The Writings of A. K. Frailey
2/9/2021

Photos speak what words no longer say,
Who once lived, loved, shaped each day.

Childhood memories,
Sweet baby fresh,
Life's possibilities,
Hope, fears mesh.

Young mother held and rocked,
Against all monsters locked.
Rustic Dad with kids did roam,
Always return, safe haven home.

In youth's mighty grasp,
The world did clasp.
Joy **overthrown**
Disappointment did own.

But down the lane,
Return hope sane,
As world jolts,

And reason bolts.

Faithful siblings clash,
Memories, tears dash.

Relentless fail,
Laughter hail.

New vision dear,
Selfless cheer,

For others,
Brothers
Sisters

Beyond touch,
Memories clutch.

Hearts swell and break,
Love—for goodness' sake.

Souls Do Matter
Originally published on
The Writings of A. K. Frailey 2/23/2021

Once upon a time-ish,

An ancient voice did call.

Men before God responded, collecting a mighty
haul.

Ever the saintly clad, reason so assured,

You got what you deserved, from every evil cured.

In stages God did send,

Our lives in newest trend.

Listen, hear, behold,

How many times must you be told?

Summer sun, glittering glow,

Frosty chill, blowing snow.

A thousand words—nature's parables did cry,

Spirits recognize passion with a lofty sigh.

Forgive them, Lord, they know not what they do.

Honesty, I wonder, have they ever had a clue?

Lie to me, with me, through me.

Despite deceit, your friend I be.

Except in the end,

Spirits break—not bend.

Between beast and divine,

Arms open wide—Yours and mine.

In our glory, fools shatter.

In perfection, our souls do matter.

God's glory do we seek,

In nature, human, divine, He speak.

Timeless, Eternal Word,

Soul's longing cry,

Finally heard.

Where Life United
Originally published on
The Writings of A. K. Frailey 3/9/2021

Your eyes record a different world than mine,

Without my music, books, or time.

Declining years loom ahead,

Your face lights with futuristic hope instead.

Joking, you say, go back to days long past,

But no return would I gladly clasp.

Childhood bittersweet,

Adolescence confusion reaped.

Love and marriage replaced dreamland,

Hard work on every hand.

Lonely passages and dangerous curves,

This present life, opportunity serves.

So many have gone before,

Some certain few stand at the door.

Tree branches end in buds to bloom,

No matter the change, it comes too soon.

Young eyes with wonder see and decide,

Old vision dims with ancient grief abide.

Hardly knowing what you don't know,

Ever and anon, it's ever so.

Look and see,

Live and be.

One day plighted,

Where life united.

Love dares,

Vision shares.

Perspective

Originally published on
The Writings of A. K. Frailey 3/23/2021

There is a vulture circling overhead,

I wonder—why can't it be a sparrow instead?

The drier signals come-get-me-now with
demanding beeps,

I tell the dog, "Go get the clothes." She
blissfully sleeps.

Sink clogged; floor sogged,

Land bogged; mind grogged.

Willow-whisps of complaint flitter through my
head,

Think of kindness, goodness, gratitude instead.

At my feet, a robin does bounce,

Upon the unwary worm, it doth mightily
trounce.

Not at a river bed beat the clothes clean do I,

Many manage still, with only a sigh.

Too much water, wrong time and place,

Try a desert for a change of pace.

Not-a-worm, labor-hunched, or on a barren site,

A change of perspective does lighten my plight.

The vulture swoops away.

Clean laundry in drawers stay.

Water drain,

Mind sane.

Rest is best.

Soul's Amen
Originally published on
The Writings of A. K. Frailey 4/6/2021

A spider web in the branching trees,

Sends winking glints in a gentle breeze.

What an intrepid climber you be,

Forever free!

My little friend may claim great might.

Above the landscape, amazing height.

Birds flutter in anxious haste,

You watch in expectation, not a breath of waste.

My admiration grows as few compare,

To tread your glorious, climbing dare.

Until I ponder your daily meal,

No breakfast, lunch, or supper there you steal.

Perhaps the same we live,

For beauty, our souls we gladly give.

But when it comes to food to eat,

From ordinary lives do we retreat.

Clouds and rain reprimand,

Hunger and thirst do demand,

A small corner on a dark day,

A quiet spot without sun's glinting ray.

Nourish the body and climb again,

For the spirit needs glory, the soul's amen.

Wait a Bit

Originally published on
The Writings of A. K. Frailey 5/18/2021

Snow fell on the green grass,
Yesterday

Apple blossoms shivered in frosty coats,
Last Night

Misty wisps covered the fields,
This Morning

Chill winds fluttered over fresh leaves,
At Noon

Sunshine and showers blessed the garden,
Evening Bliss

Forecasters hint at weather,
Tomorrow

If you don't like it,
Now

Just wait a bit.

Yet Another Day

Originally published on
The Writings of A. K. Frailey 6/1/2021

Exorbitant fear dooms all,

In gloom see nothing but a fall.

Dear spirits above holding tight,

Overcome tragedy strong-willed might.

Fragile flowers do harsh winds face.

Honeybees against storms do race.

My roots dig deep to foundation core,

Faith holds me, feeds me from an ancient store.

When the light dims and fear overshadows all,

Casting webs, terror's pall.

Hold on.

Breath deep.

To thy senses keep.

Prophet's dire warnings, cruel words spew.

Tree tops to roots, malfeasance hew.

Trust is chosen.

Beyond all hope,

Faith and charity do elope.

Impossible tomorrow,

Where the future lies,

Abiding in grace, terror flies.

Believe in that which no eye can see.

This world or the next, our lives will be.

Today fear has its say.

Tomorrow's yet another day.

If Trees Could Talk

Originally published on
The Writings of A. K. Frailey 6/15/2021

If trees could talk,

What would they say?

If they could walk,

Would they also play?

Leaves tremble in silent breeze.

Their colors change, as seasons please.

Fruit for the plucking.

Bees—nectar sucking.

Giants with myriad homes,

Rest for the weary soul.

Hewn down.

Unable to escape—fire, flood, disease...

Yet in their shadowed glen

A piercing light, God may send,

Peaceful repose.

Quiet thought.

Still abode.

Without words,

My thick-trunk friend may speak,

Livingness in green and gray.

Playfully taking me places,

My feet may never dwell.

A spirit's deep wishing well.

Nocturne Blest
Originally published on
The Writings of A. K. Frailey 6/29/2021

As the sun drops beyond the horizon low,

Leaving the crimson world aglow,

I stand alone between flowers and trees,

Soaking in a gentle breeze.

Fireflies twinkle in fairy-land darts,

Easing mind, soul, and heart.

In noontime heat,

I stroll the familiar beat.

Stepping around molehills and brushing off flies,

I pant with weariness, daytime sighs.

Just by chance,

The wind sent the oak leaves to dance,

Revealing my friend hidden beneath.

Magic in miracles of light-dance, I hold belief.

Glorious is the sudden understanding, truth,

My little friend stays hidden all day, aloof.

Faithful in habitual flight,

Enjoying the security of solitary night,

His daytime sojourn rest,

Ensures my nocturne blest.

To each own a day and night enlighten.

His to rest and then to roam.

Mine to love and hope to brighten,

Our shared home.

A Pinnacle

Originally published on
The Writings of A. K. Frailey 7/13/2021

Icy cold drink on a blistering hot day,

Cracking open a story,

to mystery glory,

Twists and turns on the way.

Chattered conversation in hearing range,

Familiar family, comfortable exchange.

Band-aids for when the peeler strays

Crunchy salad with soft bread,

Ordinary days—punctuated with holidays.

A gaze held with meaning; you know.

Relationships despite skirmishes manage to grow.

Babies, eagles, and kittens,

Platypus ridiculous, even minnows and jellyfish,

Make no moment worthless.

For in treasuring each,

The soul does reach,

A pinnacle,

To wave life's flag of joy.

Where to Feed
Originally published on
The Writings of A. K. Frailey 7/27/2021

A hummingbird flitters by,

The glittering feeder gone dry.

Guilty, I note,

Unwholesomely, upon my feathered friends, I dote.

To watch and claim my own wee-beast

I succor them from best to least.

A flighty friend, too, am I,

To wander hungry, expectations sigh.

Where to feed,

To fill my need?

The easy sugar-treat

Weakness does entreat.

Culinary goodness command,

Time, patience, skill demand.

Does the tiny bird entreat?

"Don't follow me to water-sweet.

Rather look and seek,

Nature's blossoms—humble, meek."

The shiny bottle drained.

All manner of creatures claimed.

The fake and unnatural retreat.

Their honest virtue must compete.

Plant flowering bushes to abound!

Nectar options our homes surround.

Seek not the easy life,

Without work, sweat, and myriad-strife.

Fly to that which our Creator did intend,

Our wills to bend.

To humble flower from the Earth grows true.

Or from emptiness, we shall rue.

Stop and Listen

Originally published on
The Writings of A. K. Frailey 8/10/2021

So rarely heard the common sounds

Of life that abounds.

This world in mystery,

Wrapping present into history

Leaves rustle in the breezes,

Breath of life from summer heat seizes.

Moss mounting on a branch,

Cicadas swaying as they dance,

From shells.

Distant bells,

Harmonize religious fervor take

Dogma and replace a soul for God to slake.

A yearning cry we want not to hear,

Yet with relentless hurting, message clear.

Be still and face the music

Kind and crass

Bold and beautiful

Full of wrath.

Listen

Nothing else but hear.

Creation's song.

Aching longing.

Hearts breaking.

Souls mounting.

In such union,

Is our communion.

Shimmering Green

Originally published on
The Writings of A. K. Frailey 8/24/2021

Summer leaves alive with shimmering
green,

Or scarlet with autumn's glory sheen,

Evoking mysteries yet unseen.

From inside my human-made abode

A window peers into nature's road.

Smooth floors, paneled walls, wood fans cool,

Heaters and blankets hold back winter's
fierce rule,

Protection and comfort—from a human tool.

Yet from safe indoors my soul still climbs,

Out the window to the horizon line.

As perfect as humanity can be,

My heart yearns for more than what eye can see.

Messy network of bended branches,

Squirrels scampering here to there.

A spider dances.

In webs made of air,

Creatures dare,

To live

Perpetually at the whim and providence of Him—who gives.

Safe in tight, worlds planned, unreal in reality,

We lose our hope in what might be.

To dare to dream,

In life unseen.

Where we are one with shimmering green.

Bow Thy Head

Originally published on
The Writings of A. K. Frailey 9/7/2021

Humble understanding thy limits make,
Profound reason for honesty's sake.

The soil seems simple at first glance,
But with myriad life, it does dance.

Head held high, shoulders back,
Our vision-focused, true sight we lack.

So certain sure,
We can endure.

Rain and winds, seasons galore,
Our own devices, we adore.
Then lightning strikes,
Poison bites,

Miniscule microbe,
Virus vice-hold.

Warriors' frenzy,
Leaders' envy.

Chaos.
Amid tears, the hard ground softens,
Broken hearts.

Not from lofty heights does reason rule,
But from gravesides where our grief may pool.

The Masters of our fate?
No more the ant picks death's date.

Ozymandias Ruler of All,
Time did decree—all kingdoms fall.

Faith *in* God no bargains' decree,
The faith *of* God—Move mountains, see.

Worthless pagan self-made faith,
Tempter of a demented wraith.

In God Alone,
Humbled Humanity,
True Glory Forever Shone.

Seeds of Tomorrow's Day

Originally published on
The Writings of A. K. Frailey date unknown

Saving grace of lives well lived,
Do faithful offerings make.
Far away from familiar love,
A libation for my sake.
Weakened desire
Burns fresh anew
At the temple of my need.
Kindness forges strength,
In the spirit of good deed.
Exile in life
Partner in strife
Wandering
Free.
Family ties replaced
Reformed
Chosen dear
Paths made clear.
Death has no hold when life beyond limit grows.
Blessed are the merciful, for mercy they shall
know.
We sow in fresh-turned clay,
The seeds of tomorrow's day.

Unlikely Dreams

Originally published on
The Writings of A. K. Frailey date unknown

An old day in a new week.

Slanting shadows aspirations seek.

Find endurance through counted time.

Lists and plans accounted mine.

Yet, no future eye can see—

Chirping birds insist, "Just be."

Lonely through love.

Stretching wholeness from above.

Leaves dance in an evening breeze.

Twirling, swaying, few eyes do see.

Conversation, laughter in the next room.

Me, myself, and I cocooned

Can strength be found in a new day bright,

When shadows loom and limit sight?

Who knows what tomorrow will bring?

Listen, birds, let weary hearts sing.

For hope does dwell in unlikely dreams.

Light or shadow—nothing is as it seems

Muse

Originally published on The Writings of A. K. Frailey date unknown

My friend and ever yet my enemy,

A hope-filled universe you offer me.

But of every joyous ride,

There is another, darker side,

Never real,

Forever sealed.

Once imaged, flesh and blood disperse,

No hope to rehearse,

A lovelier, honest version be,

But never an eye to see.

You loose the bonds of life,

Without a moment's strife.

Never seen upon the stage,

Neither gladness nor in rage,

Once imagined,

Fantasies are never born,

Never to laugh or to scorn.

Merely disintegrate as vapors in the sky,

I need not ask the reason why.

A truth, a fact, in reality,

So contrary,

To fulfill.

I must live authentically—still.

Servants of All

Originally published on
The Writings of A. K. Frailey 9/21/2021

Hints of pending change,

Reminding wanderers of seasons' range.

We think we know,

Sun, rain, sleet, and snow.

Unthought of winds carry hellish

storms to the door.

Thoughts crowd into actions—

Reactions Roar.

Yet when a timid vine with blossom blue

winds up the rail,

All blusters sail.

Stilled by soundless certainty,

Happiness meets joy in perpetuity.

The perfections of simple beauty—

A man's able strength,

A woman's gentle touch,

Children's innocent play,

The frogs' night chorus,

A deer feeding across the way...

Unexpected truth alters,

Our design

Our challenged wills falter,

Mysteries combine.

Warnings and hints of come what may,

Yet never is, as we say.

See the terrible and tremendous both,

For in honesty lies our growth.

Not gods with plans in hand or

self-made giants we,

But servants of all, in humanity.

In Being Myself

Originally published on
The Writings of A. K. Frailey 3/4/2022

There is an honest joy,
In being myself,
And no one else.

The excited hound,
Running through splashing creeks,
By evening, at my side, ever found.

Warbling birds, scurrying squirrels, buzzing bees,
Return home again in nestling trees.

Swirling snow and pounding rain upon the earth
Feed the soil where new life gives birth.

Farmer, Teacher, Planner, Mom,
To each, a portion of the day's work be done.
Rising and setting, no one controls the sun.

Imaginations' surmise wild new truth,
Seeing vistas beyond all proof.

Glory lust and Pride's must,
Peace lost and joy turned to dust.

Stray from each dutiful day,
Every human grief must pay.

Clean laundry folded, floors swept,
Lessons taught, records kept,
Meals holding body and soul together,

Prayers offered each evening, forever.

There is fruitful joy in being myself,
And no one else.

Warm the Cold Soul

Originally published on
The Writings of A. K. Frailey 4/1/2022

Frosted windowpanes offer no view,
Though sunshine sparkles and swirls
in hidden images.
Make of them what we do.

Incense from censers rise,
filling sacred space with muted light.
While melodic chants lift souls from solid earth to
Heavenly glory.

Whitman, Teilhard, poetic spirits join in ecstasy,
Lives chosen, insisting, no fault,
no sin in thought or word,
Though deeds may speak another creed.

From ancient battlefields, generals, politicos,
commentators, writers, actors,
musicians, artists, and clowns,

All

Proclaim Truth:
This is who we Are
Who We Must Be.

Yet

In Birth unchosen
Life demands.

In Death unwanted

Judgment commands.

Frozen sparkles give way to raindrops.
Sunlight works its will.

Mighty as we think we be,
Flesh enmeshed, bone, blood marrow,
to dust we do return.

Teardrops blur the landscape
As frosted windows melt.

Wretched ever in ourselves
Human glory deceives.

Where not the light,
Through swirls, dimly we perceive.

The mysterious veil melts away,
Evil, guilt, and pure hearts glare in day.

Tears of humility,
Penance,
Warm the cold soul.

Lush grows the
Garden.

A Spring Day.

A Land with Opposing Suns
Originally published on
The Writings of A. K. Frailey 4/29/2022

A sleepy cat requires a pat upon my lap today.
His gentle purr makes me stir.
Gladly, I give way.

Far across a sea, a land near you maybe, a
woman shrieks in agony.
On someone's command, her home, her land is
blasted beyond all memory.

Warm bread in the oven bakes.
Roast and rolls, drinks and cake, for a happy
home's sake.

Down south in weary heat, a man drags himself to
bed.
Cold-hearted brutes follow, and danger looms
ahead.

Singing birds warble good night while frogs
chorus a song.
I say goodnight to the world in which I and misery
belong.

Grief and death visit, dashing intended mirth.
Yet spring buds open, and new life gives birth.

How can two exist as one?
A land with opposing suns!

Ever it has been and ever it shall be.
One life upon the land—but joined upon the sea.

Cry and scream at unfit fate when
our turn at tears does rise.
For though we may enjoy a brief respite, on
Earth—every person dies.

Only beyond mortal eyes, do we see
across the sea,
There lies a home for all, in our humanity.

Suns become one, and whole becomes our soul.

The Problem with Evil
Originally published on
The Writings of A. K. Frailey 5/27/2022

The problem with evil is that it is.

Barnacles on ships, rot on trees,
Broken promises, all God sees.

Hidden away in my garden of ease,
I do what I must and mostly I please.

Myself.

Happy in calm and quiet
Simple life, balanced diet.

Green leaves sway in the light of day.
Birds sing and puppies play.

Startled beyond all reason why,
Bad news hurries fear, till all joys die.

Drama, trauma, crime, and greed,
Pain, suffering, lamentation seed.

Other selves love does touch,
Not myself alone, not so much.

Evil finds a way,
Through darkness to the brightest day.

Terror seeming all powerful,
To hearts most sorrowful.

Then a gentle breath breathes,
New life in spirit, hope beyond hope, now believes.

The garden awaits and birds must sing.
Distant church bells steadfast ring.

For though evil is,
It is not All,

For we are His.

The Spirit

Originally published on
The Writings of A. K. Frailey 6/24/2022

No need of wings, the spirit fled,
Among the trees, fields, and cityscapes, it tread.

Purpose-filled yet not in haste, it pursued its cause.
For though God's own mission direct, vibrant purpose
carved inner laws.

The babe it met in a cradle secure,
Yawning, stretching, life waiting to endure.

To baby eyes, the spirit could appear,
A friend, a counselor, a fairy-dear.

Many bright bird-song mornings the child and spirit engaged
In playful loving God's glory; His beauty always amazed.

Night brought comfort as both would snuggle safe together,
Dreams mere echoes of enchantments in every weather.

Toddler, child, and youth behold,
Growing at a gallop, burned fingers, singed feelings, needs
must scold.

From halting steps to pounding pace,
The spirit hurried in their race.

Aware of sadness creeping in,
Distance, abruptness, flaming cheeks, mind's worst din.

Though at his side, the spirit stayed,
The youth no longer notice paid.

65

Invisible and alone.
No seasonable music played, rather discontent, discord
grown.

Guard it would, though guide it should.
Insistent, irreverent, the man on his own stood.

Mighty and wonderful are the works of God.
But business, industry, human achievements do men
applaud.

Yet still, the spirit stayed close at his side.
Own mission broken would not abide.

Silent, secret, a friend in truth.
No less faithful to man or youth.

Time ran by and years mingled,
Warning bells rang and rumors tingled.

Aching joints and slowed pace,
No longer running, long-lost the race.

Men age in youth reverse.
A spirit's blessing, a human curse.

As he sat on a bench wood encased,
The spirit trembled close, no longer chased
Away.

With eyes now dim and hearing slight,
Perceptions strengthened in spiritual might.

Once again united, the man and spirit in companionship
found,
The breath of God's blessings safe and sound.

Rest

Originally published on
The Writings of A. K. Frailey 7/22/2022

Can words speak for a soul asleep?

Monsters convey the fears of day?

Nature's glory proclaim joy without name?

An exhausted soul drags itself to a

clearing place and stops.

No further thought compels action or attention.

Can Do No More.

The earth multitasks, spinning and revolving.

Birds chatter and sing.

Sunshine pours light and warmth from an open sky.

Conversations murmur.

Laundry swishes amid suds,

and dinner thaws on the counter.

But the soul is silent.

Asleep in dreamless rest.

Purpose laden with meaning lies not in doing.

All The Time.

Being alive is poetry unto itself.

A story's breath.

The quiet before the violin rises to meet the high note.

No prince to kiss the spirit from death to life.
No heroic clarion call echoing through the hills.
No deceptions worth believing.
For what comes next is not yours to say.
Empty and alone, quiet, and unmoving.
Death has no hold.

Banish fears in not-your-own-glory.
For today, you must rest.

Flicker of a Fairytale
Originally published on
The Writings of A. K. Frailey 8/19/2022

The flicker of a fairytale catches my eye as it wanders
across a golden meadow,
Into an enchanting woodland.

My weary soul yearns to follow.

Yet as a ladybug flitters up the summer screen, entrapped
by the scent of open air,
So, I must stay here, now, and live honestly.

A small opening, I make, for the harassed critter to try.
But its confusion is complete, never daring to dream of an
unseen hand that finds a way,
Where no way was possible.

Overwhelming work, niggling worries, sharp words, and
putrid passions
Hurry my steps through sunlight hours.

Night dreams bewilder and bother with juxtaposing
images, wonderful and terrible.

I sit at the window where late summer breezes promise
autumn beauty and comforting coolness.

Storybook perfection in colored leaves of
crimson and gold.
Not today…but soon…

From that hope-filled joy, I pull the screen aside
and shoo the ladybug,
Where it would not go but wanted to go.

It lives scant days more.
My autumn pleasure will be the death of it.
Though not today.
Today it lives a creature's mite in our mighty world.

The breeze stirs the leaves and whispers my name.
An unseen hand opens my soul,
Calling me beyond screens and all entrapments.
My life—lived with compassionate love—is a fairytale
written by an Almighty Hand
That shoos me where I would not go but want to go.

Longing for a few seasons more,
Yet flying toward an eternal land.

Nourish Life Mysteriously
Originally published on
The Writings of A. K. Frailey 9/16/2022

Majestic, snow-white, mountain-clouds edged with wispy gray threads morph across the world-encircling sky. Ever changing—bulging, slimming, rounded knobs towering into the blue, twisty peaks reaching like skinny fingers for the endless expanse across our glorious upper landscape.

Fronds of black-green plants prickle the window box, overlapping tiny round tendrils and wide palms, each demanding their share of today's life-light.

Outdoor bush cousins wave bent hands from aged branches, while young, deep-green trees belly laugh, their shimmering middles in constant, fluttery motion.

A wind chime tinkles a repeated refrain, high-toned, melodic, yet solemn as a church bell in response to the native call—nature's current, billowing breeze.

Chirping crickets, humming cicadas, warbling birds, and a single droning bee beat late summer drums, hinting of autumn, warning all who will listen—change is coming.

Scent of breakfast sausage, eggs, and toast lingers in the air, wafting between the outgoing perfume of a musician off to play the poignant organ hymns for a funeral Mass.

Spicy tea offers quiet joy to the mid-day palate, enticing happy memories to rise from the messy bed of worldly concerns.

Snappy thoughts rampage across the soul from last night's dream-delirium to the morning's first ringing phone call, questions need answers, requests demand decisions, plans must be organized, and hopes rise and fall in perfect irregularity.

To see. To hear.

Smell and Taste.

Nourish Life Mysteriously.

Inward look, silently listen, breathe hidden scents, and savor the moment.
Abundant offerings so often missed.
Beauty swept by.
Natural symphonies ignored.

Wafting scents spiral away.
Subtle flavors gobbled and gulped.
Moods erratic for no known reason.

The sun descends, the clouds converge, lightning flashes catch the eye, thunder rumbles, exciting spirits.
Fierceness makes us pause.

To see and hear, smell and taste the warning in the air.

Day does fade, and night will rise.
In cycles for a time.

Until the end.
Then silence and stillness reign.

We are left to single me.

No landscape to repair the barren desert of life unlived.

Yet, the sun does shine, a wispy cloud floats by, soon to fade, a white heart in a blue field, amid a world that can see, hear, smell, and taste life's glory—if it will.

A Ray
Originally published on
The Writings of A. K. Frailey 10/14/2022

Past voices speak to future selves in
Eternal Day.

In eager sunlight, minds divide,
separate and alert,
Made of clay.

When darkness covers all, we fall prostrate;
Union has sway.

Hybrid creation—human stature,
divine destiny—Come what may.

Are we choices, chance, spirit, or mere DNA?

Struggling to comprehend a million tragedies.
Who can say?

In the gloom of mourning, weary-soul
weakness, a cry from beyond,
Belay!

Compassionate understanding, glimmers of
truth, the light of hope,
Mock every cliché.

Souls must transcend the moral zombie zone
caught between extremes,
Hurray?

Judge not lest ye be judged,
yet decisions must be made,
Today.

There is a thread that twines us all
—good, evil, middling too,
Our part in the relay.

Ignorance and innocence, not knowing
what we know,
A gateway.

Humility and Humanity,
Love's clearest voices yet,
Will you gainsay?

The voices that ring truest, do not speak but cry,
Must devastation rule our day?

Creation we did not, though create we may,
Lies deceive with broken truth,
All betray.

In that endless end and powerless power,
Another Voice rises, a growing harmony,
Convey.

In our moment now, I speak to you,
Between ancient old and newest new,
A ray.

I pray.

Beware, Prepare!
Originally published on
The Writings of A. K. Frailey 11/11/2022

Beware Prepare!

Winter deep and long sleep,
From duty calls to heroic falls.

Clouds have assembled,
Armies resembled.

Spring long gone,
Summer's lost song.

Sweaty, twisty, grinding path that led you here.
Stop, look up, consider dear.

A touch of unseasonable, unreasonable warms the skin,
Fools the eyes,
Bewilders.

But Wilders are on their way.
Biting cold and blinding snow.
Frozen earth where nothing can grow.

Screeching winds howl warning.
Thick nests in tremulous trees joining.

Nurture within a quiet space.
Bundle soft blankets in a protected space.

Dig deep. Dig in.
Ponder. Reflect.
Await.

Only so far, the soul can go.
Frozen waterways no longer flow.

Our future dims in twilight.
Haunting past, hearts contrite.
Solace in acceptance, forgiveness highlight.

Moment by moment, the Eternal Now.
A promise, hope, dream, and vow.

Pain is no sin but teaches truth.
Aching hurt to interior growth.

Be no fool under a blue sky.
Winter can kill, and people die.

Repair your nest
And prepare your mind
Honor your soul
And guard your kind.

For this season, too, will pass along.
Stay alive to live spring's dawn.

Computer Christmas?

Originally published on
The Writings of A. K. Frailey 12/09/2022

In a midnight sky,
Announcing glorious news—low and high!
Amid glowing starlight,
Weary hearts see a joy-filled sight.

Always on,
Never dawn,
Blinking sigh,
On a blank screen go by…

Wisemen traveling to the King of Kings.
Camel bells chime and ring.
Woman blessed.
Fiat confessed.

Glazed eyes surf the net.
Nothing of interest, no, not yet.
Media trends for glory spot.
Newsy news and messy rot.

A baby's birth, man-divine,
God's holy, mercy sign.

Nano-bytes and techno-bits,
Humanity's no match for
bots' mighty hits.

Never silence in the night.
Longing for peace, a familiar plight.

Triune God in family,
Humble servants' harmony.

Selfless love,
From Above.

Strangers in person
Snapped relationships worsen.
Nowhere left to go.
Hate fills in from far below.

A touch of Grace
Slows the pace.

Peer not out–but in–and see.

Not progress in technology,
But Christmas as it should be.

Winter Stillness Without
Originally published on
The Writings of A. K. Frailey 2/03/2023

*Robin and his mate perch on snowy branches, amid
the quiet landscape.
The pond, white-crusted, a skating
rink might make.*

*Ice-laden pines pierce the frosty sky.
A distant, mystery dwelling, forever reaching high.*

*Three steps snow-mounded,
untouched by man or beast.
Serve only a reminder of lazy,
summer porch days, always facing east.*

*Hazy hang the stars, blue and purple glories,
beauties to enthrall.
Reflections, white upon the icy water,
amazed to see one fall.*

*The cabin stands serene.
The glowing window speaks, someone therein being.*

*Rich wood logs, sturdy bulwark against
the fiercest storm.
Chimney smoke rising,
wafting away forlorn.*

Is a friend inside? Is it someone that I know?
My heart yearns to inquire, knock upon the door,
unheeded by the snow.

Separate souls across the way,
the seat across the aisle.
Marching down the street,
distance increasing by the mile.

Who are you, Other? The one I cannot name?
We live upon the Earth, today,
living much the same.

Mr. Robin and his mate,
Watch in accepting fate.

Not alone, yet lonely,
Wondering who you be.
I am on the outside, loving the scenery.

About the Author

A. K. Frailey, an author of a historical sci-fi and science fiction series, short story collections, inspirational non-fiction books, a children's book, and a poetry collection, has been writing for over ten years and has published 17 books.

Her novels expand from the OldEarth world to the Newearth universe—where deception rules but truth prevails. Her nonfiction work focuses on the intersection of motherhood, widowhood, practicing gratitude, and rediscovering joy.

As a teacher with a degree in Elementary Education, she has taught in Milwaukee, Chicago, L. A., and WoodRiver, and was a teacher trainer in the Philippines for Peace Corps. She earned a Masters of Fine Arts Degree in Creative Writing for Entertainment from Full Sail University.

Ann homeschooled all eight of her children. She manages her rural homestead with her kids and their numerous critters. In her spare time, she serves as an election judge, a literacy tutor, and secretary/treasurer of her small town's cemetery.

Made in the USA
Middletown, DE
24 October 2023

41335402R00051